Weather Patterns

Monica Hughes

Heinemann Library
Chicago, Illinois

Customer Service 888-454-2279
Visit our website at www.heinemannlibrary.com

Editorial: Jilly Attwood, Kate Bellamy
Design: Jo Hinton-Malivoire
Picture research: Ginny Stroud-Lewis, Ruth Blair
Production: Séverine Ribierre

Originated by Dot Gradations Ltd
Printed and bound in China by South China Printing Company

08 0/ 06 05
10 9 8 7 6 5 4 3

Library of Congress Cataloging-in-Publication Data
Hughes, Monica.
    Weather patterns / Monica Hughes.
        p. cm. -- (Nature's patterns)
    Includes bibliographical references and index.
    ISBN 1-4034-5881-2 (HC), 1-4034-5887-1 (Pbk.)
    1. Weather. I. Title. II. Series.
    QC981.H85 2004
    551.6--dc22
                                        2004000938

Acknowledgments
The author and publishers are grateful to the following for permission to reproduce copyright material:
pp. 4, 5, 6, 13, 15, 18, 19, 22 Corbis; p. 8 Richard Klune/Corbis; p. 14 Mark A. Johnson/Corbis; p. 16
Time Page/Corbis; p. 17 Getty Images; p. 20 Charles O'Rear/Corbis; p. 21 Alamy; p. 23 Image Bank/Getty
Images; p. 24 Ray Juno/Corbis; p. 25 Gunter Marx/Corbis; p. 26 Oxford Scientific Films; p. 27 Galen
Rowell/Corbis; p. 28 Noaa; p. 29 Mike Chew/Corbis

Cover photograph is reproduced with permission of Corbis.

Our thanks to David Lewin for his assistance in the preparation of this book.

Contents

Some words are shown in bold, **like this.**
You can find out what they mean by looking
in the glossary.

Nature's Patterns

Nature is always changing. Many of the changes in nature follow a **pattern.** This means that they happen over and over again.

In some storms, there is a pattern of lightning and thunder.

Sun and rain may create a rainbow.

Different parts of the world have different weather patterns. Some weather patterns happen every day. Some weather patterns happen every year.

A Pattern Every Day

There is a **temperature pattern** that happens every day. It is cool in the early morning, warmer toward **midday,** and coldest at night.

This temperature pattern happens because Earth is always turning. Places are warm when they face the Sun. They get cooler as they turn away from the Sun.

A Pattern Every Year

Most places have a yearly weather **pattern,** too. They have the same weather at the same time each year. The different times of the year are called **seasons.**

The weather is warmest in the summer.

Yearly weather patterns happen because Earth moves around the Sun. As Earth moves, some parts are nearest the Sun. Some parts are farther away.

Climate Patterns

The weather **pattern** that a place has is called its **climate.** The climate is linked to heat from the Sun. The Sun's **rays** bring heat to Earth.

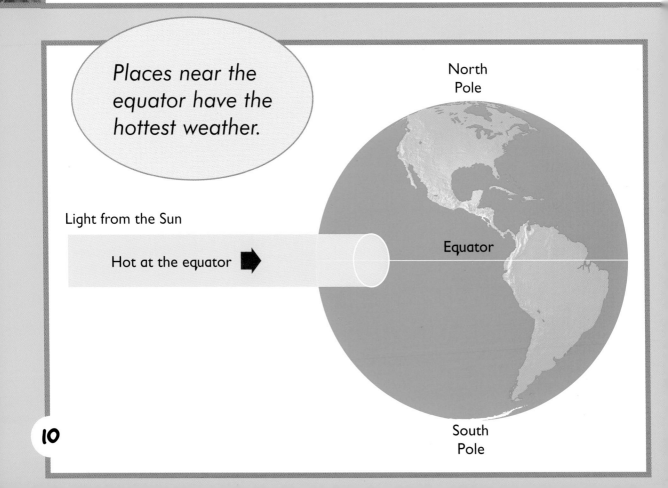

Places near the equator have the hottest weather.

North Pole

Light from the Sun

Hot at the equator

Equator

South Pole

Around the **equator,** it is hot all year. At the equator the Sun's rays hit Earth straight on. The Sun's rays are strongest when they travel straight down to Earth.

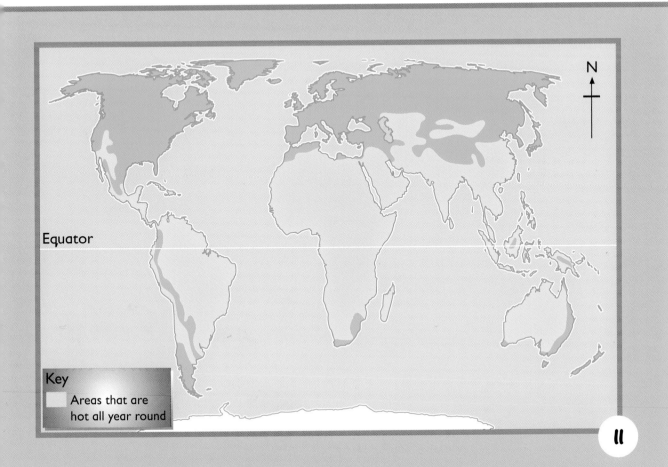

N

Equator

Key

Areas that are hot all year round

Different Climate Patterns

Climate patterns are different around the world. Away from the **equator,** the Sun's **rays** do not hit Earth straight on. They hit Earth at an **angle.**

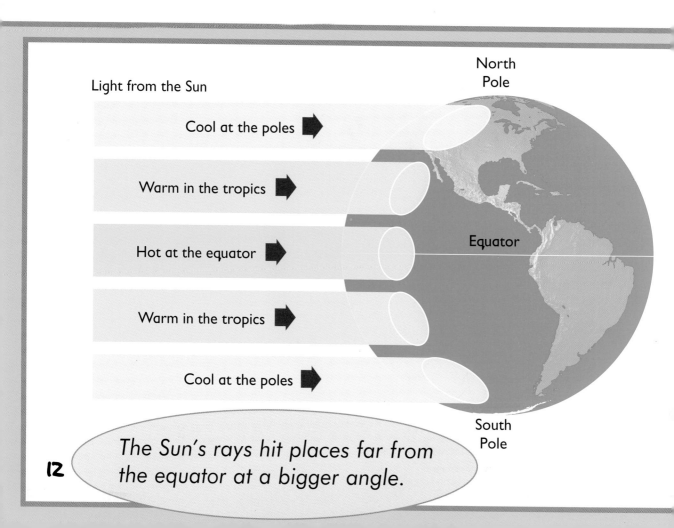

Light from the Sun

Cool at the poles

Warm in the tropics

Hot at the equator

Warm in the tropics

Cool at the poles

North Pole

Equator

South Pole

The Sun's rays hit places far from the equator at a bigger angle.

When the Sun's rays hit Earth at an angle, they cover a wider area. The heat is not as strong.

At the poles the Sun's rays fall at a large angle. These places are cold all year round.

13

Hot and Wet

Places closest to the **equator** do not have different **seasons.** These areas have a **tropical climate.** It is hot and wet all year round.

The hot, wet climate of the rain forest is good for plants.

Most rain forests have thunderstorms and heavy rain every afternoon.

Rain forests have a tropical climate. They have the same **pattern** every day. Night is cool, and the morning is hot and sunny. Clouds form during the day, and rain falls in the afternoon.

15

Dry and Wet

Some places with a **tropical climate** are hot all year but have two different **seasons.** Half of the year it is dry. During the other half, it is wet.

Storm clouds gather at the start of the wet season.

The wet season can begin suddenly with heavy rain and strong winds. This rain and wind is called a **monsoon.**

Monsoon rains can cause flooding like this.

Hot and Dry

Desert areas around the **equator** are hot and dry. They have a daily **pattern** of very cold nights and hot days.

A desert's wet **season** may be short. If there is too little rain, the desert has a **drought.** A drought can last for months or years.

When there is no rain, the ground dries and cracks.

Seasonal Patterns

Some parts of the world have four different **seasons.** Spring is warm. Summer is hot and sunny. There is often very little rain.

Warm climates are good for growing fruit.

In some places, it rains in winter, but it is not very cold.

Fall is cool, but winter is **mild.**
Winter has more rain than summer
but not much frost or snow.

21

Different Seasonal Patterns

In other places, each **season** has a different kind of weather. Fall is cool and wet. Winter is long and cold with frost or snow.

In some places, special trucks clear snow from the road.

Lambs are born in spring.

Spring and summer have higher **temperatures** and less rain than fall and winter. Summer is hot.

More Seasonal Patterns

Places far from the **equator** have a colder **climate.** These places have a short spring and fall. Summer is also short but can be hot.

Summer lasts for about two months in cold climates.

Winter is long and very cold in places far from the equator. Winter days are much shorter than summer days.

The winter is so cold that lakes and seas freeze over.

Polar Patterns

The North Pole and the South Pole are farthest from the **equator.** In these places, summer is very cold. The Sun is low in the sky. The ground stays frozen all year.

The North Pole is in the Arctic, and the South Pole is in the Antarctic.

Winter at the North Pole and the South Pole is long and very cold. Strong winds and snowstorms are common.

At the poles in winter, there is little daylight.

What Will the Weather Be Like?

The weather **patterns** in a place help people **predict** what the weather will be like there. Predicting the weather can help us decide what clothes to wear.

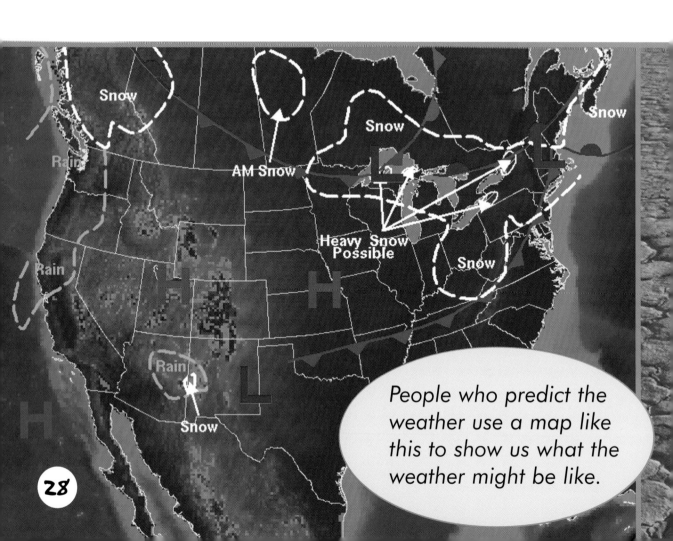

People who predict the weather use a map like this to show us what the weather might be like.

Predicting the weather helps people know where to go for winter sports.

Weather patterns help us know when and where there will be snow. Weather patterns also help us know when it will be hot and sunny.

Look for a Pattern

Use a thermometer to record the outside **temperature** every hour for two or three days. Pick the same place every day and make sure it is not in direct sunlight.

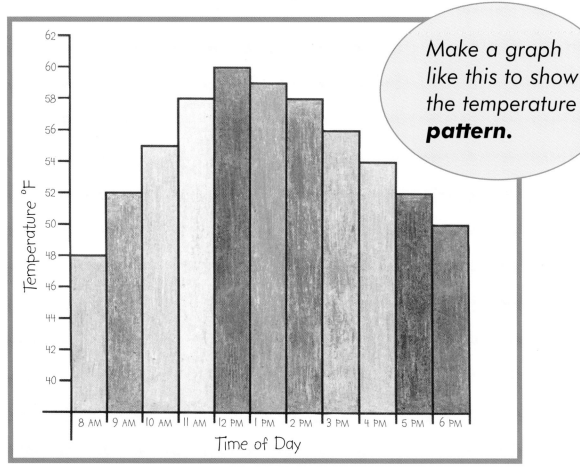

*Make a graph like this to show the temperature **pattern.***

Glossary

angle way something slopes or slants

climate usual weather pattern of an area

desert dry, sandy area with little rain

drought time when there is no rain

equator imaginary line around the middle of Earth

mild neither too hot nor too cold

midday noon; the middle of the day at 12 o'clock

monsoon season of heavy rain and wind

pattern something that happens over and over again

predict to say what will happen in the future

rays lines of sunlight

season time of year. Each season has a special type of weather and temperature

temperature how hot or cold it is

tropical a very hot and rainy area

More Books to Read

Christian, Sandra J. *Meteorologists*. Mankato, Minn.: Capstone, 2002.

Hewitt, Sally. *Weather*. Danbury, Conn.: Scholastic Library, 2000.

Wallace, Karen. *Whatever the Weather*. New York City: Dorling Kindersley, 1999.

Weber, Rebecca. *Weather Wise*. Minneapolis: Compass Point, 2002.

Index